Oceans

by Anna O'Mara

Bridgestone Books

an Imprint of Capstone Press

Facts about Oceans

- Oceans cover more than two-thirds of the earth's surface.
- The oceans contain 97 percent of the water on earth.
- The world's biggest ocean is the Pacific Ocean.
- The smallest ocean is the Arctic Ocean.

Bridgestone Books are published by Capstone Press • 818 North Willow Street, Mankato, Minnesota 56001
Copyright © 1996 by Capstone Press • All rights reserved • Printed in the United States of America

Library of Congress Cataloging-in-Publication Data
O'Mara, Anna.
 Oceans/Anna O'Mara.
 p. cm.
 Includes bibliographical references and index.
 Summary: Provides basic scientific information about oceans including their size, floors, mountains and mid-ocean ridges, trenches, volcanoes, currents, tides, and waves.
 ISBN 1-56065-339-6
 1. Ocean--Juvenile literature. [1. Ocean.] I. Title.
GC21.5.058 1996
551.46--dc20

         95-47653
          CIP
           AC

Photo credits
FPG International: 4. Scenics, ETC.: 8-14.
J.P. Rowan: cover, 16-20.

Table of Contents

Words in **boldface** type in the text are defined in the Words to Know
section in the back of this book.

One Big World Ocean

The biggest bodies of water on earth are oceans. They cover more than two-thirds of the earth's surface.

The oceans contain 97 percent of the water on earth. The rest is found in glaciers, icecaps, lakes, rivers, under the ground, and in the air.

The waters of the oceans form one big world ocean. The continents divide the ocean into parts. They are the Pacific Ocean, the Atlantic Ocean, the Indian Ocean, and the Arctic Ocean.

Some scientists count only three oceans. They think that the Arctic Ocean is just the top of the Atlantic Ocean.

The Antarctic Ocean covers the bottom of the earth. It is not really an ocean. It is the bottom of the Atlantic Ocean, the Indian Ocean, and the Pacific Ocean. The Antarctic Ocean is also called the Southern Ocean.

Oceans cover more than two-thirds of the earth.

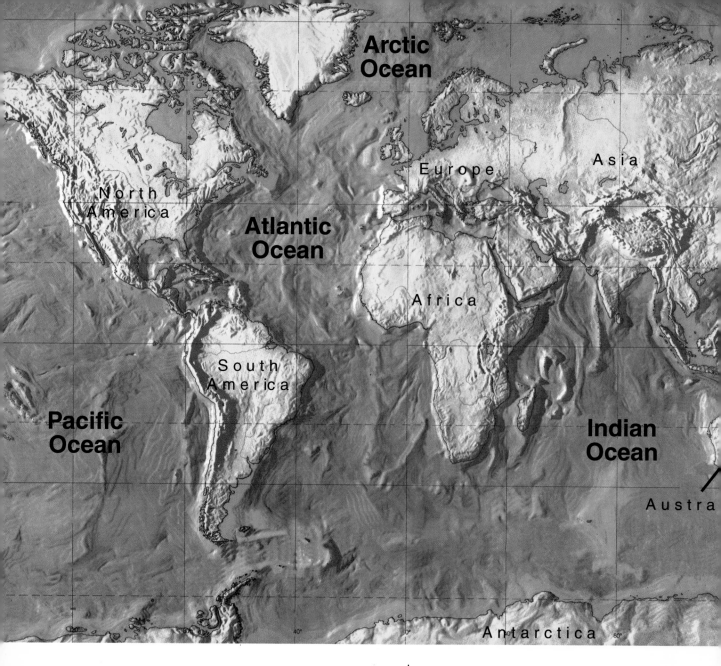

Oceans of the World

The Biggest Ocean

The world's biggest ocean is the Pacific Ocean. It reaches from North and South America to Asia and Australia.

The Pacific Ocean covers nearly one-third of the earth's surface. It holds almost half of the water on earth. It is so big that the other oceans could fit inside it.

The Atlantic Ocean is the second biggest ocean. It reaches from North and South America to Europe and Africa.

The Indian Ocean is bordered by Africa, Australia, Indonesia, and Asia.

The smallest ocean is the Arctic Ocean. It is at the North Pole. Ice covers most of this ocean.

The average depth of the oceans is 2.3 miles (3.7 kilometers).

The Ocean Floor

From the shore, the ocean bottom gradually slopes down. This is the continental shelf.

The water gets deeper as this shelf goes farther into the ocean. At the deepest part of the shelf, the ocean is 660 feet (198 meters) deep.

The continental shelf may go out as little as one mile (1.6 kilometers) into the ocean. Or, it may go out more than 100 miles (160 kilometers).

At the end of the continental shelf, the bottom of the ocean suddenly drops away. This is the continental slope. This slope is steep. It drops down two to five miles (three to eight kilometers).

The ocean's floor lies at the bottom of the continental slope. The floor is not flat. Mountains rise up from the bottom. Deep **trenches** cut into the floor.

The gradual slope of the ocean from the shore is called the continental shelf.

Mountains and Ridges

Ocean mountains look like those on land. Most are completely under the water. Some rise above the surface.

Mauna Kea is an old volcano in the Hawaiian Islands. From its base on the ocean floor to its top, Mauna Kea is almost six miles (9.6 kilometers) high. It is the highest island mountain in the world.

Chains of mountains run along the floor of the oceans. They are called **ridges**. Most of the tops of the ridges are about 1.5 miles (2.4 kilometers) below sea level. But some tops rise above the surface. Islands like Iceland, the Azores, and the Galapagos Islands are the tops of ocean ridges.

The longest ridge is the Mid-Atlantic Ridge. It is in the Atlantic Ocean. It is 10,000 miles (16,000 kilometers) long. There are deep valleys in these mountain ridges. Some of the **canyons** are as deep as the Grand Canyon in Arizona.

The highest mountains in the world rise from the ocean floor.

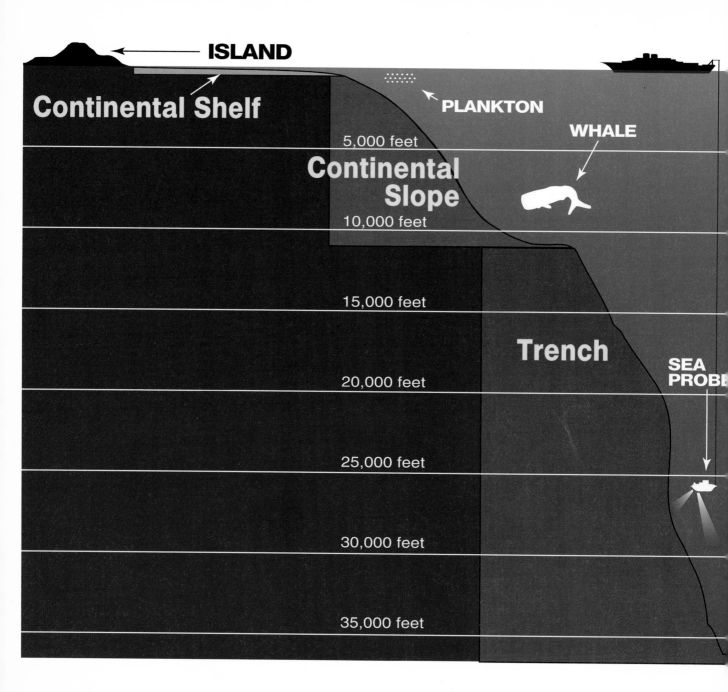

ISLAND

Continental Shelf

PLANKTON

WHALE

5,000 feet

Continental
Slope

10,000 feet

15,000 feet

Trench

SEA
PROBE

20,000 feet

25,000 feet

30,000 feet

35,000 feet

Trenches

The oceans have deep cuts called trenches. They are long and narrow. They have steep sides that go deep into the earth.

The deepest trench in the world is the Mariana Trench. It is in the Pacific Ocean near Guam. The Mariana Trench is about seven miles (11 kilometers) below the surface of the ocean.

Mount Everest is the tallest mountain on land. It is 29,028 feet (8,708 meters) high. Imagine that Mount Everest was dropped into the Mariana Trench. It would disappear. Its top would be more than one mile (1.6 kilometers) under water.

Mariana Trench is the deepest trench. It drops about seven miles (11 kilometers) below the surface of the ocean.

Volcanoes

    Volcanoes are holes in the crust of the earth. Volcanoes erupt, or blow up. Liquid rock called lava spills out.

    Many volcanoes have erupted in the ocean. When the lava cools in the water, a mountain begins to grow on the ocean floor.

    As the volcano erupts again and again, the mountain grows higher and higher. It slowly pushes up through the water.

    When the top of the mountain sticks up above the water, it is an island. The Hawaiian Islands in the Pacific Ocean are the tops of volcanoes.

Volcanoes slowly become islands as they erupt over many years.

Plankton and Ooze

Plankton float on or near the surface of the ocean. They are tiny sea creatures. They drift with the ocean currents.

Ooze covers the bottom of the ocean. It is found in very deep water. It is made up of many things.

Plankton shells are in the ooze. These shells are a little bigger than a sugar crystal. When plankton die, their shells sink down to the bottom of the ocean. The dead plankton mix with mud to make ooze.

Red clay lies below the ooze. Rock lies below the clay. This rock is cooled **magma** that bubbled up from the center of the earth.

Sea birds feed on the creatures that float on top of the ocean.

Currents, Tides, and Waves

The ocean is in constant motion. Currents, tides, and waves keep the ocean moving.

Currents are rivers in the oceans. The wind and the spinning of the earth cause currents. These rivers move faster than the water on either side of them.

Tides are the rising and the falling of the level of the ocean. The spinning of the earth and the pull of the moon and the sun cause tides. Tides rise and fall about every six hours.

Wind causes most ocean waves. The waves move across the surface of the ocean, but the water does not move forward. The water moves up and down. The movement of the waves is like the waves made in a ribbon attached to a pole. When you shake the free end of the ribbon, waves move along it. But the ribbon does not move forward. When waves reach the shore, they break and form the **surf.**

Ocean waves are caused by the wind.

Salty Water

Ocean water is salty. A lot of the salt comes from rocks that are wearing away on land. Rain removes salty minerals from land and rocks. Streams carry the minerals to rivers. Rivers carry the salts to the oceans.

When ocean water **evaporates**, it leaves salt behind. Then the ocean becomes saltier. When a lot of rain falls, ocean water becomes less salty.

Salt is left behind on rocks and other land formations when ocean water evaporates.

Hands On: You Can Save the Oceans

People are polluting the oceans. What can you do to save the oceans? The Smithsonian Institution in Washington, D.C., has come up with several ideas. Here are some of them.

- Do not leave the water running when you brush your teeth. It wastes water.
- Do not release helium-filled balloons outside. They could end up in the ocean. They could harm animals that might eat them.
- Never litter.
- Recycle paper, metal, plastic, and glass.
- Cut open plastic six-pack holders before putting them in the garbage. If they make their way to the ocean, they can kill sea animals. The animals can get tangled in the plastic.

Words to Know

canyon—a deep valley with steep sides

evaporate—to disappear into a vapor

magma—hot, liquid rock beneath the earth's crust

ooze—dead sea life and mud that cover the ocean bottom

plankton—small plants and animals that float in the ocean

ridge—chain of underwater mountains

surf—waves breaking on the shore

trench—deep valley in the ocean floor

Read More

Goldman, Linda. *Cleaning Up Our Water.* Chicago: Children's Press, 1994.

Hoff, Mary and Mary M. Rodgers. *Our Endangered Planet: Oceans.* Minneapolis: Lerner Publications, 1991.

Simon, Seymour. *Oceans.* New York: Morrow Junior Books, 1990.

White, Larry. *Water: Simple Experiments for Young Scientists.* Brookfield, Conn.: The Millbrook Press, 1995.

Useful Addresses

American Oceans Campaign
725 Arizona Avenue
Santa Monica, CA 90401

Greenpeace
2623 West Fourth Avenue
Vancouver, BC V6K 1P8
Canada

Friends of the Earth
1025 Vermont Avenue NW
Washington, DC 20005

Hawaii Volcanoes National Park
Kilauea Visitor Center
Hawaii National Park, HI 96718

Index